COMPOSER SHOWCASE
HAL LEONARD STUDENT PIANO LIBRARY

Circus Suite

FIVE ORIGINAL PIANO SOLOS

BY MONA REJINO

CONTENTS

Editor: Margaret Otwell

ISBN-13: 978-1-4234-1140-6
ISBN-10: 1-4234-1140-4

HAL•LEONARD®
CORPORATION
7777 W. BLUEMOUND RD. P.O. BOX 13819 MILWAUKEE, WI 53213

In Australia Contact:
Hal Leonard Australia Pty. Ltd.
4 Lentara Court
Cheltenham, Victoria, 3192 Australia
Email: ausadmin@halleonard.com

Visit Hal Leonard Online at
www.halleonard.com

Introduction

I have vivid memories of the first time we took our children to the circus. It was such a joy to see the excitement they felt as each dazzling act opened before their eyes. From the plodding elephants to the amazing acrobats and hilarious clowns, we were royally entertained! My hope is that this collection of circus-themed pieces will bring back similar, fond memories for the students who play them. Enjoy!

"Clowns On Unicycles" is non-stop fun from the first note to the last. Even passage-work and careful attention to articulation marks will add to the humorous nature of these entertaining clowns.

"The Elephant Parade" requires patience and steadiness on the part of the performer. These elephants are not in a hurry, and they take everything in stride. Taking time to analyze the melodic patterns will make this piece much easier to learn.

"Tumblers" are always one step ahead, intriguing the audience with their nimble moves. Smooth hand-crossings and proper use of the damper pedal will help you give a successful performance.

"Camel Ride" conjures up images of camels on a trek through the desert. These camels have a sassy, clever personality that can easily be captured through the use of staccatos, accents, and a wide variety of dynamic levels.

"Circus Tricks" has a bouncy, rhythmic feel to it. The use of mixed meter and chromatic passages add to the carefree nature of spending a wonderful day at the circus.

—Mona Rejino

Clowns On Unicycles

Mona Rejino

The Elephant Parade

Mona Rejino

Slow Waltz tempo, with a swing (♩♩ = ♩ ♪) (♩ = 88-96)

Tumblers

Mona Rejino

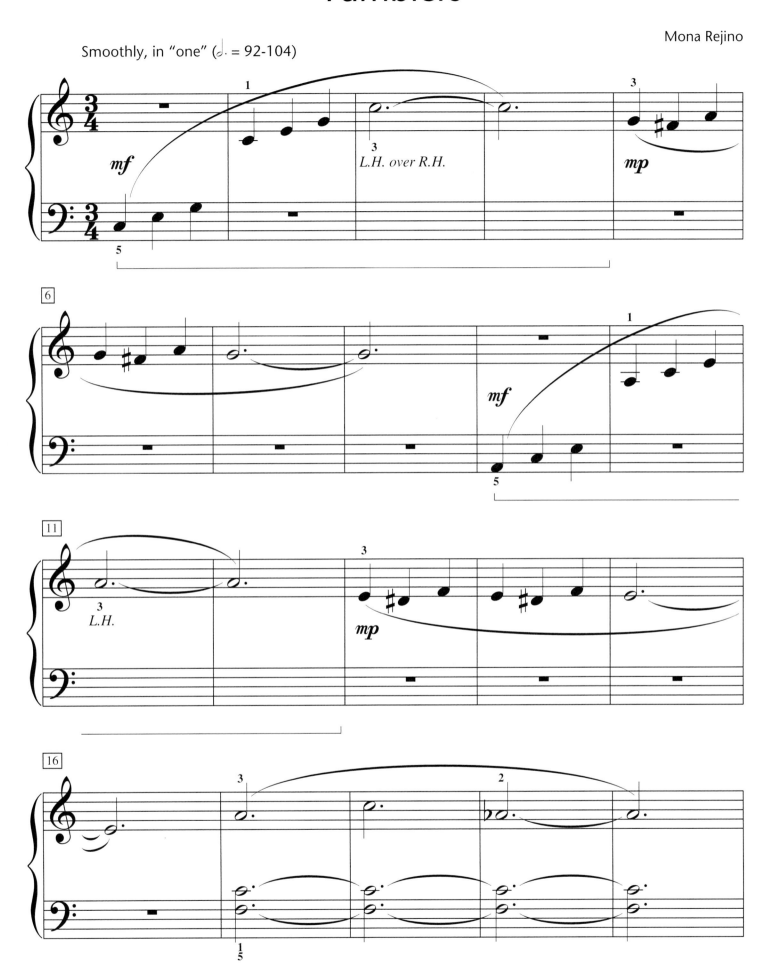

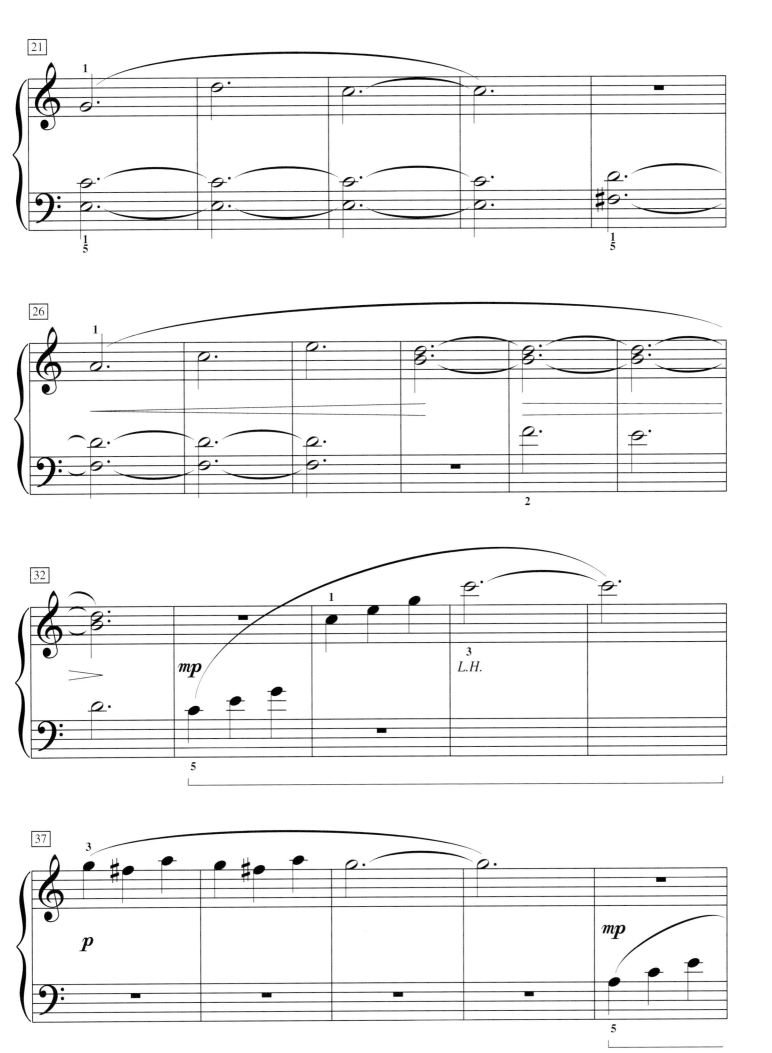

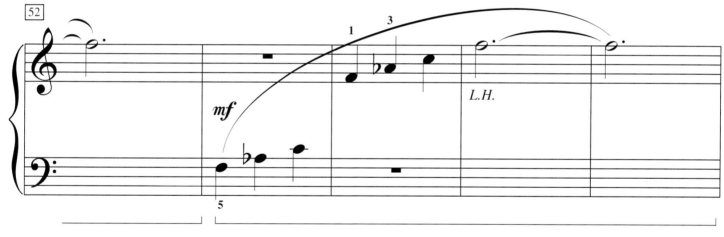

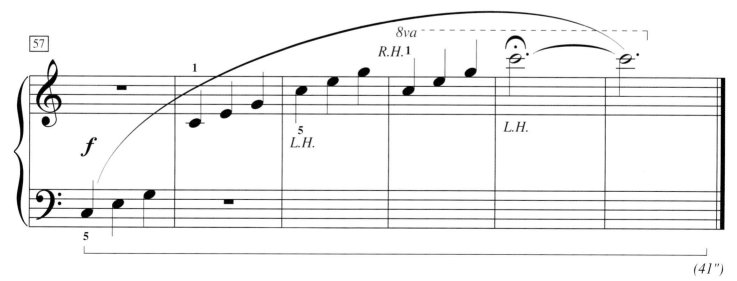

(41")

Camel Ride

Mona Rejino

Circus Tricks

Mona Rejino